RECLAIM

YOUR

MANHOOD!

BY RYAN FELMAN

TABLE OF CONTENTS

The Resurrection of the American Dream

Modern life involves journalists from failing institutions harassing men for having a political opinion openly stated on national television. College degrees are worthless or near worthless as student debt rises, while trades are lucrative, cheap to get, and looked down on by snobby city folk who favor going 6 figures into debt before entering the real world. And then they'll whine about student debt being unfair after they're given their education. Young people have grown frustrated with the status quo.

I'm one of these millennials that everyone bitches about claiming we are all lazy and I think we invented cancer when we mined all those bitcoin mountains.

Print is dead, so it's a good thing I decided to throw my hat in the ring as a writer. Maybe I'm one of the authentic writers though. I don't write for the money, but to maintain my sanity. Even though the more I write, the more I begin to question my sanity, but in the days of reality TV show Presidents and social decay, to accept the modern world as it is, is to truly be insane.

The American dream is dead, but why then does it appear to be easier than ever for many to make their dreams possible? Young people leverage the power of the internet to create their own blogs, websites, businesses and um… "modeling careers." The old world is dying as the boomers retire on the money stolen from generations before and after them, yet they still struggle to save. It can be difficult to survive on 6 figure incomes when your house is as big as your ego and your god is materialism.

Everything today is a bit too fantastical for my liking. I'm young but I feel older with each passing day. The world has been given a cartoonish filter as if we are playing Fortnight on LSD. Nothing feels real and everything is evanescent. The bottom feeders troll through digital pasts to drag down those who climb too high as if we are crabs in the bucket. This loser mentality is the only way for many to win the game, or at least to lose less. The winners sneak by but now live in fear. #MeToo and divorce threaten to undermine those who have done everything they were supposed to do.

My moment of clarity was when I was dragged through a broken family court system and forced to pay a quarter of a million dollars to a deadbeat opiate addict to ensure the safety of my son. I got my son, so the old people tell me that the system works. They don't mind the tremendous expense and toll on my personal health that this entailed.

I don't second guess them on this, because they are puppets who won't give my young mind the time of day. They know better since they're old. That is why, despite all my adversities, I still have significantly more money saved than the average boomer who worked decades longer than me. That is the key right there, isn't it? The system does work, but it doesn't work for you. The system is capitalism and it will outsource jobs to socialism if that means stealing money from a productive writer / whateverthehelliam to give to a drug addict. Now why would capitalism do this?

Because the market always wins, and capitalism knows that the money flows much quicker when taken from the highly intelligent but fiscally conservative and given to the junkie who is addicted to every quick fix known to man.

I hold no regrets nor ill will towards my ex despite the wrongdoings as it did cause me to reevaluate my own life. Since the split I created my own website, www.PathToManliness.com where I am a voice for frustrated young men in a system that depends on them while simultaneously bashing them. I tweet random thoughts of inspiration and satirical commentary to keep myself sane while providing a resource to an increasingly alienated segment of the population.

The older generation doesn't recognize the death of the old world, but I see it everywhere around me.

The circus over the Supreme Court hearing was evidence enough for most, but there is so much more destroying the American empire.

The lack of proper education and perhaps intentional destruction from Bill Gates to further his own personal agenda where he will surely make back double what he has invested through his common core scheme. The destruction of the food system to its very core. Most food is so heavily polluted with chemicals and estrogens that few men in the city can help but succumb to becoming these numales or soy boys that shout "The Future is Female" while still not getting laid. The obesity epidemic leaves few males capable of leaving much of an impact on the real world, so they retreat to their own safe spaces of drive thru windows, video games and porn. They are of little concern to those in power.

This country grows so divisive that the government is hardly relevant anymore. Men and women don't trust each other as name calling, false rape and divorce destroys the gender dynamics that led to a fruitful population. Not to mention the death and destruction wrought by endocrine disrupters and planned parenthood. If you aren't upset, you aren't paying attention. There is a very active war out there to combat overpopulation and it is working like a charm. Well, except when it's not and if you look at where we are heading, it certainly paints a picture.

The American dream is dying, but Americans don't lay down easy. The youth of America see the challenges and adversities that lay ahead, and for some, it only inspires them to become greater men. Only a small percentage of people are the true movers and shakers that shape the destiny of an empire and they may already be laying the foundation through ideas and words. Upon the creation of America, only three percent of the population fought against the British Empire. You see, I chose to become a writer because I recognize the inherent power in words, and with the rise of the internet, even Presidents can be memed into office.

I recognize the frustration and despair in many young men today and I merely offer a voice of reason and traditional values to remind them that they are not alone.

If this resonates with you, read on and take the words I offer you as advice to ensuring that your life is on the right path. Do not sleep through this life as so many people do. Take these 20 steps and implement them into your life and watch yourself reclaim your manhood.

1. Hit the Gym

Take control of your own life and make something of yourself. Get your ass in shape and build up your confidence. Buy the fast sports car. Write that book. Start your website. Don't let anyone hold you back with their self-doubt and disbelief. That is why they are average.

To pursue the life of excellence, is to reject the world of mediocre. The world of comfort and entertainment. The entertainment industry doesn't want you to push yourself. They prefer their customers to be overweight and unfulfilled. They want you to fall into a life of mediocrity as you'll be more susceptible to their advertising.

As our lives grow more comfortable, the competition seems to be getting thinner. Figuratively, not literally. I see a lot of sad and lazy people. People who are overweight, underdressed and lacking a likeable personality. This may describe you.

If you find your girl slowly losing interest in you and touching you less, hit the gym. Getting back in shape is a surefire way to rekindle the flame. Watch your girl swoon and caress your bigger muscles.

Keeping yourself physically fit affects other people's immediate perception of you, your self-esteem, and your capabilities. Do not underestimate!

Do you ever think about going home to visit childhood friends or the girl who got away?

When you go home, will you be the guy that they joke about because he let himself go and got fat, or will you be the guy that they stare at in lust or envy. This may be your motivation at the gym. Or you may simply be training yourself to be harder to kill. Imagine that one day, someone is going to kill you, or try to. Now imagine that he's not coming for one year. How would you spend your time during that year? Adopt the warrior's mindset for your own path to manliness.

Personally, I hit the gym about 3 times a week and I do a solid 45 minutes of weights with a quick cardio warmup and cooldown. For cardio, I'll alternate between jogging, sprints, biking or rowing. Now I may have only gone to the Harvard of the Midwest, which is the University of Illinois, but I do know that rowing is one hell of a good workout. Those fancy rich boys out east seem to stay in great shape by rowing crew.

Any of these exercises are adequate for getting the heartrate up. When lifting, I rarely use machines but opt for free weights because they help strengthen your stabilizer muscles. Machines are for isolation which has its purpose too. I see the machines as more beneficial for superficial muscle growth where as old fashion iron will give you real world practical strength.

As I've progressed farther on my path, I've taken to enjoy running a bit more. Believe it or not, this can happen to you too. It will take time, practice and perhaps some weight loss, but you can get there. I honestly look forward to my runs now. It is a time where I can meditate and focus on new ideas. I tend to find a local trail in the woods or run on a nearby college campus. Both offer their own scenery and unique energy that help you to focus on improving yourself.

Bottom line: If you are not in athletic shape, then that should be goal number 1 for you. Put down the potato chips and stop drinking so much beer. If you can't be disciplined enough to stay in shape, what makes you think that you will be disciplined in other areas of your life?

Adopt the warrior mindset and set out to conquer your life!

2. Dress Well

Lose the jerseys with other dude's names on them and toss out the sandals and crocs. Stick to timeless pieces that fit well. Follow Tanner Guzy and WellBuiltStyle on Twitter for professional advice.

For amateur advice, I'll throw my hat in the ring now. Feel free to skip ahead to the next chapter as there are better voices on this than myself. Let no one say that I'm not reasonable.

If you go out dressed like a slob every chance you get, you have no idea how much you are holding yourself back in life. Now I almost never wear a suit or tie, but I always look good when I step out the door. You never know who you will meet, whether it's the love of your life or the guy who will offer you an exciting business opportunity. Conversely, if you have holes in your shirt and stains on your cargo shorts, well, opportunity may pass you up because you look like a crazy homeless guy.

I once had a guy from Edward Jones offer me a job while we were waiting for beers at a bar in Chicago. I was wearing jeans and a button down, but it fit well, and it was a good solid look. Don't overthink this one. Few people take the effort to look nice, and fewer still find clothes that fit their bodies. Fit is what makes you look like a man dressed to impress versus looking like a boy dressing up in his father's clothes.

What got me the job offer was my words in our conversation, but we likely wouldn't have talked much if I was wearing a snapback and an oversized football jersey.

I wasted too much time in my youth struggling to learn fashion when I should have focused merely on style. For fashion is temporary but style is timeless. Stick with timeless pieces and your wallet will thank you. If you want to have fun and get a velvet sport coat, go for it, but I recommend getting the staple pieces first and working from there.

Staple pieces? Well if you don't know what those are, think James Bond. Even in the older movies he tends to still look presentable by today's standards. Solid color button downs with a suit will look classy long after you are dead. For more casual affairs, go with well-fitting khakis or dark jeans, dress boots and a button down. Polos are tough to pull off unless you are in great shape. I tend to save those for soccer games and golf. Roll up the sleeves on your button down if it's a bit warm. This will also give you a nice rugged look. This is especially true, if you followed the advice from chapter one!

Simple pieces that fit and are made of decent quality will always beat out the average guy at the bar, baseball field or in the bitcoin mines.

3. Be Assertive

Stand up straight. Look people in the eye. Speak confidently and slowly. Make your words meaningful and people will listen. If you can do these very simple things, you will stand out in a sea of awkward, uncomfortable men.

Young men are learning to keep their head low at school but retreat away from interaction. This is a sad cost of a school system that rewards feminized behavior. The assault on masculinity is systemic. This is but one piece of it.

Women love assertive men, not assholes. Most young guys get this conflated. How do you be assertive? A lot of it has to do with language. Stop using weak phrases such as: I just, I don't know, What do you wanna do? I'm not sure and Where do you wanna go. Women are looking for answers. Why else would they ask you a question? Be decisive and have a plan in place if you want to impress her. Even if you don't know, show confidence and tell her that it's a surprise while you quietly work out the details in your head.

As for work, well…. Which guy are you going to work with? The quiet and unsure guy who fears making mistakes, or the man who boldly takes action and provides actionable advice. Which one of these men describes me? Now I know I can make mistakes, but I've found life is much better when you work on fixing those mistakes than despairing over why you didn't act at all.

In baseball it is always better to go down swinging than to take a pitch and hope you get a walk. Bold men make bold moves. Men of action take control of their own destiny rather than hoping for change.

This is what separates the men from the boys. A man knows how to hold a conversation with friend and stranger alike. A man knows how to take action rather than be subject to the actions of those around him.

All twenty of these points build on each other as well. It may be difficult to be confident and assertive out in public when you are 50 pounds overweight. Yet as you hit the gym and take up running, you can begin to shed those pounds. As you do this, get ready to watch your confidence rise with your health.

Men don't need to hide away from the world. On the contrary, as men don't seek the validation of others if they recognize that they are doing what they feel is right. At the end of the day, what truly matters is that you, as a man, can look at that man in the mirror with pride.

4. Choose Your Friends Wisely

Get rid of toxic losers who obsess over drinking and drugs. They're holding you back. Find friends who share positive hobbies with you such as biking or a sport. Find people who are driven.

The average person is lethargic, unmotivated and depressed. They are overweight and out of shape. The average person also spends most of their nights playing video games or watching porn. They eat too much fast food and drink too much alcohol. They smoke pot, cigarettes or JUULs and none of these habits are as healthy or productive as you want them to be.

If you use most of your time to pursue a hedonistic lifestyle as opposed to meaningful pursuits, then it is no wonder you find yourself fat, lonely and depressed.

And if you consort with people with these bad habits, then you are prone to fall into the same bad habits as your friends.

Contrary to popular belief there are alternative hobbies to going out drinking every weekend. I will admit that I spent plenty of nights in college and through my twenties getting drunk at bars, and weddings, and lakes.. and even a Christmas special that a girlfriend dragged me to once. Somehow that relationship didn't work out. Alcohol makes it easier to socialize, but the quality of those relationships are seldom worthwhile.

If you want to meet people of quality, you need to find better habits and hobbies. Martial arts, the gym, hiking and running are all excellent alternatives to the bars and will improve your overall wellbeing.

The people you meet in these more respectable hobbies will be people who share a similar vision and thus be able to help hold you accountable should you start to slack. I am fortunate in that I have a group message going where we share workout advice and training programs. We did a team Spartan race together this year. No one wants to let down their teammates so all summer long we trained together and on our own to get in the best shape possible for our race. That accountability helps push ourselves past our limits.

Now I must admit that when they first proposed the idea of a Spartan Race, I initially said no. Which is very uncharacteristic of me, but I will be honest and tell you that I had my doubts. I had recently gained some weight and hated running. I told my friend, "I can't run a Spartan." To which he immediately replied, "Yes you can, because we have time to train." Not wanting to back down from a challenge, I agreed to run the race.

I had to start small, but I immediately took steps to get in shape. I ran a 5K and nearly died. I hated running so I rarely did it. But I knew that with practice and a better diet, I could change my hatred of it.

With the Warrior's Mindset, you find a way to conquer any obstacle and running was simply the next obstacle. I ran every week, twice if I could find the time. Each week I ran a little farther until I felt ready to conquer this Spartan Race. I used apps that tracked my distance and time and would push myself to run faster times and longer distances. It became a game. A race against myself and I was kicking my ass.

By the time of the Spartan Race, I could run around 8 miles which was twice the distance we would be running. I had dropped 20 pounds, which was twice my goal for the year. I was setting new personal records in the gym lifting weights. For the first time in my life, I was able to climb a rope. I regularly was doing pull ups, crunches, hill climbs, bucket carries, and I loved it all. How could I love such torture? Because it all made me the very best version of myself.

With the right group of people around you, they can become worthy assets that inspire you to become the very best version that you can be. And if you are reading this book, that is your overall goal.

5. Turn Off the Video Games

You say you have no time to get in shape, or cook a good meal, but you level up your dumb avatar in a virtual world.

You need to be honest with yourself here and there are a few touchy subjects that people will defend like addicts. Gaming is certainly one of them.

Do you spend all day at work staring at a screen only to come home and again, stare at a screen? Health aside, is this really the lifestyle that you want? Take that energy you put into gaming and focus it towards real world grinding.

Video games reward your brain with a false sense of accomplishment.

Like it or not, most gamers are holding themselves back from more meaningful pursuits. You could gain XP all weekend or you could focus on your side project. You do have a side project, don't you?

How much time did you spend last year gaming and what could you have done instead. In economics, the term for this is "opportunity cost."

Now I write fast at times, but I can realistically punch out 15,000 words in around 600 minutes. That is the length of the average E-Book. In fact, this book is about that long. Now let's add some time for editing and brainstorming; so, we can round up to about 1000 minutes. If you are spending 1,000 hours a year playing video games, you could realistically take that time and put it towards writing your own book. Many people are spending more time than that too. It amounts to less than 20 hours a week. And don't give me any excuses as I put my money where my mouth is. I used to game about that much and now I see what a colossal waste of time it was.

Today I can call myself a writer, whereas in the past I was merely a gamer. As a man who idolized Hank Moody in Californication, this is an exciting prospect for me. Now when someone asks me, what do I do, I can respond with, "I'm a writer." Even E-gamers won't get the look of intrigue that often follows that response.

Now, yes, I would like to game on occasion and I probably spend a half hour here or there, but it isn't a part of my life. I simply have better endeavors to pursue with my time.

No one ever went to their deathbed saying they wish they played more Fortnite.

The world is far too interesting if only you get off the quick fix of dopamine from gaming, porn and Netflix. Join the real world and level up your life. It will mean more in the long run and ultimately be more fulfilling.

6. Eat Real Food

Do you often find yourself lacking energy? Are you overweight? Unhealthy? Change your diet and change your life. Eat natural food like meat, veggies and nuts. Throw out the processed garbage.

To walk off a Big Mac combo meal, you need to walk 40,000 steps. The expression "You can't outrun your fork," is true for a reason. Many of the young men out there will bust their ass all week long at the gym or running before work, only to undo all that hard work by drinking 10 beers on Friday night. And then there is football… Curious how a sport that requires athleticism and healthy habits has a culture of binge drinking and overeating.

You need to stop eating processed junk and high carb diets. This will slow you down and make you struggle in the gym and on your runs. Since eating a more natural diet, I have seen my energy levels and performance spike. I tend to eat a high protein diet with as much meat as I can find. I consume lots of eggs and nuts, and a bunch of veggies. I also eat fruit so whatever you want to call it. It is close to paleo, but not 100% strict adherence to it.

To quote Oscar Wilde, "Moderation in all things, including moderation."

Most guys think its manly to pound beers all weekend, but then they can't run more than a couple miles or hammer out 25 pushups. The promotion of binge drinking as a manly endeavor is a marketing ploy to trick young men into forking over their hard-earned cash to a giant corporation.

It may have been said before, but if you get into the habit of eating better and natural foods, you'll be amazed at how well you'll feel. This improves your energy, mood and health.

Water is a big contributor here too. The sensation of hunger is very similar to that of thirst. Oftentimes I find myself feeling hungry only to watch that feeling subside after drinking a glass of water. The health benefits of water are innumerable and an easy change to make.

If you can't get your health in order, your whole life is in jeopardy of falling apart. Everything flows from exercise and eating right, and few people truly appreciate this in their lives.

7. Have Some Self-Respect

Society has attacked manliness in nearly all venues of life. Now we have a society filled with confused men who don't know what it means to be men. We have broken the nuclear family and caused a generation to be raised without a positive male role model in the house.

Stop drooling over instathots and literal whores online parading as, ahem "models." Stop paying to see online girls and go out in the real world.

Chase your goals, not girls.

I made this mistake for years. Girls can sniff out desperation from a mile away. Now, I can get a number with cold approaches, but a number can often lead to flaking out if it isn't obtained the proper way.

There are others who can tell you better how to cold approach girls, so I'll skip that for today. But if you want to learn a foolproof method for meeting girls, here is the cold hard facts. Follow the advice in this book.

Hit the gym is Chapter 1 for a reason. If you look your best, women will be naturally attracted to you. Sorry about your luck but the fat acceptance movement is likely only going to lead to you having to accept fat dating prospects. People tend to date in the same weight class. It's a bit like the UFC in that regard. And men tend to punch up a weight class on this. Excuse the expression.

If you spend months or even weeks talking to a girl and waiting for the right opportunity, it'll never happen. Strike while the iron is hot, and the best time is within the first 5 minutes. In 5 minutes the average girl will decide whether she is attracted to you or not. If you follow girls around like a lost puppy, she's likely using you for self-esteem boost and validation. Show some self-respect and move on with your life.

If you create an interesting life, women will naturally be drawn to you. Women love success, confidence and excitement. A man who focuses on his own goals and makes his mission his priority will have way more success with women than the man whose sole purpose is to chase girls or spin plates.

Sex is one of those things that is taken for granted when available and relentlessly pursued when deprived. There are better ways to spend your days, gentlemen.

Also, quit taking life so seriously. How old are you? Because you're likely younger than you think. Every year I seem to get more and more attractive. Women don't want men to figure that out. As I age, my income goes up, my strength goes up and my knowledge and wisdom go up. I've gone from broke college student to corporate drone to writer and lifestyle coach. Not to mention I have continued to work out and get in better shape each year. Men age well if they take care of themselves. Quit acting like there is this invisible deadline for you to meet the right girl. I still get college chicks to look at me doe eyed and casually initiate contact. Constantly.

If you're going on a date with your own money, do shit that you'll enjoy. This shifts the power in the relationship. Do you like to drive cars? Go to a go kart track. Want something exhilarating? Shoot guns at the range. Hiking or running. Fuck all that nonsense about going to the movies and playing mini golf. Grow up. Actually, you know what? I retract my statement about mini golf. It's still awesome. Women will respect a man who knows what he wants in life.

Whatever you do, be sure to make it exciting. She'll associate the feelings of the date with you. You need to make her FEEL something. Adrenaline, excitement, happiness. Maybe even nostalgia. None of my best first dates were at restaurants. Its cliché. DO SOMETHING. This makes you stand out.

8. Stay away from BPD (BiPolar Disorder).

Anthony Bourdain lost his life and I almost ruined mine with a BPD girl. They manipulate you into thinking that you are the crazy one. You can't fix her so don't even try. I wish someone had informed me about BPD and the reality of the disorder when I was younger. I underestimated its effects.

10 Red Flags to Look Out for in Women

These are all from my experience with women. Mostly from one woman that I spent way too much time with. I felt bad for her and bought in to this psychopath's web. This can happen to you if you don't see the warning signs! Here on the Path to Manliness, I am offering advice in helping young men live fulfilling lives and here I will help you avoid many of the mistakes I made in my younger years.

While I recognize that this chapter is available for free on my website, it bears repeating as this advice will literally save lives.

Daddy issues / All men are jerks

An obvious one but there are plenty of men who will overlook this serious red flag. This is a sign of past issues. If all men are jerks, she's the issue. There are too many princesses out there who think their shit don't stink. They expect the perfect ideal mate but can't cook, won't clean and they come with more baggage than a transcontinental flight. But at least they have debt from their worthless liberal arts degree!

A poor role model in a father will lead to a woman not knowing what to look for in a man. She holds resentment towards all men because her initial experience with a man (her father) has tainted her perception. It can be hard for these women to get over past issues as she has been conditioned to think that all men are like the men in her past.

Obsessed with Social Media.

This is a big one! If she can't stop staring at her phone, that means she craves attention and validation. She likely has a huge following of losers who will feed her attention when her self-esteem is low.

She may also be using you for housing or money while she searches for a better option. Men are comfortable being alone, whereas women crave validation and attention. They struggle to be alone, even if it means they must settle temporarily. This is how sexless marriages happen. Understand that Disney and society has sold you a lie and that not all women are honest princesses. There are plenty of great women out there, but there are also manipulative snakes who will play with your emotions and your ego.

Messy Car/ Room = Messy Life

If she can't be bothered to keep her room or car clean, what makes you think she will be able to keep her life in order? This type of woman will bleed into your life with her messy habits. Both literally and figuratively. How a person, whether it's a man or woman, treats their living environment is a sign of discipline and work ethic. It doesn't have to be spotless, but this is a warning sign that she may have depression or other issues that prevent her from cleaning up who own space.

Guy Friends

This is an obvious one, but young guys somehow overlook this all the time. The average male friend is too chickenshit to ask a girl out, so he is content to be nearby. Most women know this, but they love the self-esteem boost from the attention.

If you get into a fight with your girl, be prepared for her to run to one of her guy friends. She will do this to get a reaction out of you and to make you jealous. Or she will go out to the clubs with them. Walk away from the relationship. I'm dead serious on this one and in the heat of the moment, it will be easier said than done, but the short-term pain is nothing compared to the long-term ramifications.

Cut your losses and walk away from the relationship.

This is a lack of respect and a man worth his salt will not tolerate this type of behavior. If you allow her to walk all over you at the beginning of the relationship, you will have no say once she locks you down in a marriage where she'll be able to threaten divorce, 70% of which are initiated by women. They are economically incentivized to do so.

"I don't like to talk about my past."

Alright, what the fuck does that mean?! Were you a stripper? Prostitute? Slut in college? Drug addict? You'd be amazed at what some girls will hide from you and they will see nothing wrong with it in their minds. They will rationalize their behavior with comments like, "I was a different person then."

Disassociation from reality is a sign of a psychopath. Stay away. I fucked up big time on this one. Never again. If they are uncomfortable with their past, be weary of the future. Past results are indicative of future occurrences.

Drugs

STAY AWAY from junkies! A little pot and booze is no big deal. Moderation is fine. But if she was into hardcore stuff or had a habitual habit, this is 100% a deal breaker every single time. No arguments. No exceptions. Block her number and move on with your life.

It is insane what a junkie will do, and you do not want to be a part of the experience at all. In my experience this is a lifelong problem for many and the odds of finding someone who doesn't relapse is not great. This goes for pharmaceuticals too. Many women out there are addicted to legal drugs or are chemically unbalanced, so they are heavily medicated on legal drugs. They will make you think that you are a psycho.

Excessive Cleavage and Skin (Ass Seems to be More Popular These Days)

Social media has bred the most decadent and immoral generation of women that have walked the face of the Earth. 99% of you all are not fucking models. You belong in Hustler, but most aren't attractive enough. The problem with social media is there are no barriers to entry and the masses reward the asses. Hence the rise of "models" who are posting pictures of their ass for validation.

Women who post slutty pictures online are low value and emotionally broken people. If they must flaunt skin to get attention, it is likely indicative of having nothing else to offer. Narcissism is not a hobby.

Shopaholic

Shopping is not a hobby It is a waste of time and practiced by materialistic and shallow people. Those who shop all the time have too much time on their hands and no purpose in their life. Obviously, these women will drain you of funds. Too many men today buy into the lie of society that men are supposed to provide everything for women, while women are also supposed to be equal. You can't eat your cake and have it too.

Lying

This includes little white lies (so much for white privilege). People who lie are hiding skeletons in their closet. Don't let curiosity get the best of you. Block and move on with your life. It is also a sign of a psychopath.

BPD - Fuck Your Feelings

I dated two girls that had BiPolar Disorder. I didn't understand with the first one until years later. The second one hid it for a long time. This is hard to explain, but BPD is contagious. They will make you feel like you are the psychotic person by turning their issues around on you. You will get into fights over petty issues and everything will be your fault. BPD women have a knack for conditioning men to alter their behavior. It will take time and effort to undo all the damage.

The difference between a Bipolar Disorder and psychopathy is a very thin line. They are chemically unbalanced, and the mood swings will be all over the place. It is like living with multiple women who look identical. You will never know who you are talking to. Avoid at all costs.

9. Stop Being Stingy

There is no shame in being frugal, but there is a difference between frugality and being cheap. Being frugal is growing your food or cooking at home, whereas being cheap is tipping 5% because you couldn't afford going out to eat in the first place.

Tip well. If you can't afford to leave a good tip, then go to a cheaper restaurant, or eat at home. These people are working hard and if this a place you frequent, they will treat you better or worse depending on how you treat them. The golden rule applies here.

Dress well. I covered this earlier but being stingy applies to yourself as well. In college I bought a cheap pair of sandals for $15 every summer. They would fall apart before Fall every year. Then one day I spent $45 on a nice pair of leather sandals. I have them today, 8 years later. Going the cheapest route is not always the cheapest route in the long run. And more importantly, people will be judging you based on how you look.

Another perfect example is people who refuse to replace a car. I'll bet you have a friend who brags about the car that he owns outright and doesn't have to make payments on it. The problem is that this car keeps breaking down and he has essentially replaced the car payment with a maintenance payment. And on top of that, his choice of transportation is unreliable. There is a certain piece of mind that comes with a car that will consistently shuffle you from place to place. Now I'm not saying to go buy a brand-new car, but there is a happy medium between living large and being a cheapskate.

The grocery store is another tricky place. Don't get me wrong. I'm not saying that everyone should eat Filet Mignon every night, but your health needs to be priority number one. Most people can find places to cut back on other than the grocery store. If you are penny pinching at the grocery store, you are at jeopardy of putting your health at risk. Most cheap food is not healthy, but it doesn't have to be terribly expensive either. Do yourself a favor and buy real ingredients and learn to cook. You can afford decent food if you stop picking up fast food and drinking ten beers on the weekend.

Eat well. Drink well. Buy better and buy less. Quality over quantity. Become a connoisseur, not a mindless consumer.

There are a bunch of dudes out there who bought into the media's lies that it is manly to pound beers all weekend, but they can't even run more than a couple miles or hammer out 25 pushups. The idea that overindulging in beer is masculine is a marketing ploy to trick young men into forking over their hard-earned cash to a giant corporation. And yes, that is the second time I've said that because it needs to be hammered into your head until it is engrained in your memory!

If you are going to drink, drink with a bit of class. Enjoy a local IPA or better yet, a glass of good bourbon. Be sure you don't overdo it and show your ass.

10. Stop Buying Soybucks Milkshakes

These drinks that claim to be "coffee" are fat, soy filled, diabetes factories. I saved you $5 a day thus about covering your cost of this book.

Real men drink real coffee, not this new age milkshake garbage that is popular with college coeds who simply want to drink coffee and pretend like they are adults. You want to be drinking like your Grandpa, not like Becky.

Making coffee is not that hard and the average cup of coffee bought at retail is around $5. Which sounds cheap but really a daily coffee is costing you $1,825 a year. Not to mention the time and gas you waste going to the coffee shop.

If you must go buy a cup of coffee, at least support your local small business when you do so. Where I live, the local brew is significantly better than the franchise coffee shops and the atmosphere is much more personal.

This goes back to the eating real food chapter. You need to change the way your mindset works with diet. A child chooses what they consume by seeking out sweet and tasty treats. A man considers food to be fuel and his body to be the machine that runs on it. By being more mindful of what one puts in their body, you can keep that machine running more efficiently. Most of what goes in these milkshakes that people call coffee is horrendously unhealthy, especially to start off your day.

And if you are that much of an addict to your coffee drinks, perhaps you should reevaluate your sleeping schedule. Most people aren't getting enough sleep. I understand how busy we can all be, but your health depends on getting a good night's rest. If you are wasting time at night playing on your phone or watching junk TV, consider that this time could be spent better. Whether that means getting to bed earlier or using an hour or so to wind down before going to sleep.

Electronics give off blue light and it throws off your circadian rhythm. Rather than watching TV, playing video games or perusing your phone, try to write or read a book before bed. This will help improve your quality and quantity of sleep, and then coffee can be a fun way to start your day rather than a necessity.

11. Be Resilient

A man is tough and can take the punches this life gives. Failure is a learning opportunity on the way to a life of excellence. Show me a man that never fails, and I'll show you a man that never pushes the envelope.

The most pivotal moments in my life revolved around failures. These moments guided me on my path into becoming the man I am today.

It is never too late to change your life. What can you do today to improve yourself? Be persistent and militant with this change and you won't recognize yourself in one year's time.

What separates excellence from mediocrity is that persistence. Mediocre people will try a new habit but give up too quickly. You must remain persistent over weeks or even months before you begin to see results. This is true with weight loss, exercise, writing and nearly everything in your life.

So many men will make great strides of progress and then let it all fall apart when life throws a hurdle at them. I've been guilty of this myself. In the past I would make excuses like "I'm in my busy season at work," or "I have too much stress in my life right now."

Then I went through a brutal divorce and found out the true meaning of busy season and stress. You know what else I discovered? That all those excuses were a bunch of bullshit keeping me weak. During the most stressful and busy time in my life I hit the gym multiple times a week with no excuses. I would work out and talk to my lawyer at the same time on occasion. I also was raising my son and I took up writing during this period of my life. Though I had plenty of tasks to occupy my time, I was simply spending my time much more productively.

It is in these moments when you need your mental and physical toughness the most. The truly resilient man recognizes that mental toughness is nothing without physical toughness. And vice versa.

Life is going to throw adversity at you. How you handle it will define your resilience and your true character.

The older I get the smaller my problems seem. I remember getting upset about a $900 auto repair bill in my early 20s. Earlier this year I had an unexpected maintenance bill for $3,000. The $3,000 bill bothered me less than the $900 bill. Yes, I'm making more money now, but I've also changed my mindset. In the grand scheme of things, these hurdles don't really matter. They are part of life and that means you must prepare for life's little emergencies.

The average American is living by the skin of their teeth going paycheck to paycheck. But they aren't working on a side gig to supplement their income. They have the sports package on their TV and spend too much time and money on drugs or alcohol yet complain that they can't seem to get by. These people will sooner take handouts than give up these little pleasures that they feel entitled to. Reclaim your manhood and prepare for your own future.

Part of the issue here may be that you or these people aren't pushing themselves at work. So many will clock in and clock out, doing the bare minimum. If you are willing to go the extra mile, it puts you well above the average worker.

12. Jobs Aren't Hard

I understand that for many people, their job is simply a paycheck, and not a passion. Every day, I see people doing the bare minimum at some shitty job and you can tell they hate it. They probably think the work is beneath them. There is nothing wrong with thinking that as it is often the truth.

Saying that you deserve a better job doesn't mean anything though. The trick to bettering your career is proving it by going the extra mile. You never know who will notice you on the right day. Take pride in your work ethic.

Show up on time. Don't do drugs and be positive in your attitude and manner of speaking. People enjoy positive mindsets and want to be around positive people. Do this and it will put you in the top third of the workforce.

I had a boss at a previous job tell me that if they were to drug test the workers in the factory, they'd lose about half of their workforce due to controlled substances. This is your competition. So, if you have the self-control to not do drugs at work, you are already ahead of the curve.

Do you enjoy your job or at the very least gain satisfaction out of doing your best work? This puts you ahead of another chunk of the average workers. Key word there is average. How often do you hear people say they hate their job, or that they can't wait until Friday? These are people who do the bare minimum and clock in and out as fast as possible.

All you must do is put forth an honest effort and show a little passion in your job, and you'll be recognized for it. The problem is that so many people expect instant recognition. It may take months. It may take a customer seeing how hard you work and how attentive to detail you are. This customer could be your next employer.

You never know who you are going to meet and when you will meet someone who has the power to change your life. You never know when one of these people may offer you the chance of a lifetime. If more people shared this mindset, more people would be able to pull themselves out of their mindless job and find themselves moving up in the world. But if you spend your time at your job doing minimal work, you shouldn't be surprised to wind up with minimal rewards to show for it.

Now everyone works a shitty job at some point in their life. I've done backbreaking labor out in the fields, but you know what? I enjoyed parts of that job. I was outside in the fresh air and I was getting exercise. Focus on the good parts of the job and be mindful of learning opportunities. Even the worst job could be a helpful experience later in your journey. That backbreaking job was good ammo for me in future job interviews.

Painting, bailing hay, landscaping… I've worked plenty of jobs that some would say are beneath them, but there is no shame in honest work and we all start somewhere. The issue with many young people who struggle to get the job they want, is that they expect to be given giant responsibilities with little to no track record. Those jobs I worked as a teenager were helpful references later in life when I applied for more meaningful jobs.

It is a huge risk for a business to hire a young college educated employee who has never worked or has poor experience. Therefore, learning how to sell is an essential skill for everyone! If you don't know how to sell yourself, how will anyone know that you are worth their time and money? If you don't learn how to sell, you'll likely be underemployed.

13. Stop Watching Porn

It is a waste of time and its fucking up your mind. It gives you a false sense of accomplishment. Make yourself a better man and go out in the real world to find a real woman.

Porn is the easy way out. Video games are fucking with your reward system by making you chase virtual accomplishments instead of real world pursuits. In a similar fashion, porn is fucking with your brain by allowing you to take the easy road as opposed to seeking out a meaningful relationship and true human intimacy.

Your brain craves accomplishments and gaming and porn give your brain a false sense of accomplishment. Living a life of overindulgence in gaming and porn will lead one to a depressing life. While in the moment, you may be having fun, it ultimately will leave you with shame and a lack of pride in yourself.

Creating a meaningful life involves having a winner's mindset. This means pursuing habits of value rather than hedonistic vices that offer short term enjoyments.

Now many will say that modern women are whores, but they refuse to acknowledge the possibility that they are looking in the wrong places. The bar is a great place to meet friends and watch the game; it is rarely the place to meet high quality women. Not only that, most men waste their time on gaming and porn rather than pursuing a truly interesting life and staying fit. This puts them at a huge disadvantage for two reasons. One, they aren't in shape and give off a bad first impression before they even open their mouths. Two, they spend too much time online and have little of interest to share in conversation. They are stuck in a loser mentality.

Every incel is only one gym membership away from meeting women in the real world.

Many young men who obsess with gaming and porn, are simply frustrated with job prospects and dating prospects. And the gaming and porn often do go hand in hand. Enough hand stuff. How can we fix this?

This book is your handbook for straightening out your life so that you can live a more fulfilling and ultimately enjoyable life.

Get yourself to the gym and find more meaningful hobbies. Getting outside to walk and hike is a great way to start your fitness journey if you aren't ready for a full tilt workout.

Now many people are missing meaning in their life and gaming can fill that void. But its unhealthy and leads to looking less attractive. I know it's not impossible to be a gamer and stay in shape, but you need to be honest with yourself here. If you can't find the time to keep yourself healthy, you need to accept the fact that gaming is holding you back from taking care of your body. This leads to a lack of good dating prospects, and then men turn to porn out of frustration. It's a downward spiral that can be very difficult to escape from.

14. Start Writing

My life really began to improve when I started writing.

It is a great habit to learn more about yourself and to delve deep into your psyche. It will keep you sane. My writing developed over time, but I'll admit I had humble beginnings. There can be a progression to it.

When I first started out, I wrote in journals. I would do this almost every night and now I rarely go anywhere without bringing a notebook and pen with me. A gentleman keeps a pen and notebook on him.

At first, all my writing was relegated to that notebook, but soon it progressed to tweets. The journal helped me practice as my early writing was unrefined and often chaotic. Tweeting allowed me to get my thoughts out in the real world and test the waters. By tweeting thoughts and ideas, you are given instant feedback while simultaneously sharing insights and wisdom with other fellow human beings. Twitter, when used correctly, can be a valuable resource. Later in this book, I have great advice on how to grow your own Twitter account.

Now as I began to get a pulse on what young men were interested in and what they were missing in their lives, I formed my website and began to post my thoughts and findings in more well thought out and coherent writings.

Progressing further still, I have taken what I have learned from tweeting, from writing on my website and now it has culminated in this very book that you are now reading. What is important to takeaway here is that anyone can do this. I've given you a nice outline here to get started.

Write in a journal. Tweet thoughts and ideas for instant feedback. Write posts on your website. Formulate your writing and create more content to construct your book.

If you stay persistent in your efforts and provide value, you will be successful.

A true writer knows that inspiration can strike at any time. Be sure to be ready to capture those thoughts as they can be fleeting.

If I can help it, I keep my trusty Field Notes notebook and a nice quality pen on me always. Why do I opt for an old fashioned physical notebook when there's an app for that? First off, it is 100 times more gratifying to cross off a task using a physical pen and an actual notebook. If you don't believe me, try it.

Secondly, it is nice to class it up a bit with a tried and true method that your grandfather would approve of.

Third, when the Chinese set off an EMP and the guy next to you loses all his writing when his laptop is fried, you get to look awfully smug as you continue writing as if nothing ever happened.

The world is growing more artificial and virtual by the day. While I do enjoy reaching great minds and engaging people on Twitter, there can be a point where too much of our lives are virtual. Balance, in all things.

Why should you get a quality pen?

I thought it was silly for the longest time that people would buy a pen. People are giving away pens like it's a young dweebs virginity. Please, will someone just take it! At my old job, they had a room full of them and I would grab a couple for work, and a couple for home.

Then I had a coworker mention to me how gratifying it is to use a quality pen that costs a few bucks. Since I am a writer now, it feels appropriate to have the right tools. I use a pen every single day at work and it is frustrating when it doesn't write perfectly. So, I took the plunge and bought a $7 pen. It was a Parker Jotter retractable ballpoint pen.

First off it looks amazing and feels amazing. It is smaller than most pens which makes it easier to carry. It even feels of higher quality as it is made of metal as opposed to plastic, so I don't fear it snapping in my pocket when I sit down. I now own about a half dozen quality pens that I keep in various places: my desk, my car, my laptop bag, etc.

A gentleman is always prepared, and as this gentleman has officially become a writer, it is imperative that I be ready to jot down notes and ideas.

Despite humanity becoming cyborgs who are inseparable from their phones, we need not rely on these machines for everything. A notebook has a longer battery life than any smartphone. Also, if one is a tough masculine man who can defend himself to reasonable avail, the idea of hacking a notebook is more challenging. Come dox my field notes!

How many times do old people give you a hard time for looking at your phone? My girlfriend jokes with me all the time that I'm on Twitter too much; sometimes she may have a point. Still I've found a wealth of wisdom on there as well. There are many instances in your daily life where glancing at your phone is perceived as rude, and this is perfectly understandable.

Like wearing a watch, a notebook is a refined and tasteful way to jot down the odd thought or idea that enters one's mind. You'll find people are not only less annoyed at the sight of a notebook, but even intrigued, for it is the mark of a man with purpose.

If you struggle with focus and staying disciplined, the notebook will help keep you on task. Writing down notes on your phone can be interrupted by texts, notifications or phone calls. Not to mention all the apps on it vying for your attention.

I also keep a couple of the larger Moleskin notebooks at my desk to do some late-night introspection. It is not unusual for me to start jotting down some random thoughts only to later have them develop into a full-blown post for the ole website. I usually end up having to elaborate a bit as I can be terse in my journal as my mind seems to move faster than my pen, but the core point I'm trying to make is often made on paper first.

A man who doesn't take a few moments each night to evaluate his direction and purpose in life is a man who is at the mercy of other influences. I have found great truths to myself and the life that we live by taking pen to paper. It has also allowed me to keep track of my goals and notice what is working, and what needs tweaked.

By physically writing down my goals this year, and checking on them periodically, this has been my most productive and thus, satisfying year I have ever had. There is something to be said about writing things down. By having a tactile object in the real world, it makes the idea more concrete.

When you look around in public and the plebeians all have their nose down in their phones, stand apart by using something that is real. In a world gone digital, sometimes the old-fashioned ways are the more satisfying and fulfilling methods.

Life hack: Before you go to bed, grab a notebook and write your reflections on the day, or the weekend. Explore your thoughts on your day. What lessons did you learn? What can you improve on? What are your goals and how are you working towards accomplishing them? Set up a game plan for the week ahead.

15. Goals

Rather than having an abstract idea or vision in your head, you need to make your goals real. Write them down. Check them periodically to assure that you are making progress toward your overall mission. Stick with them and write down specifically how you will accomplish them.

In ancient Sparta, the people were expected to earn their citizenship. You weren't born a Spartan. You had to earn the right to be called a Spartan. This rite of passage, called the agoge, began at 12 years old and was an arduous task, sometimes taking the lives of these boys in the process. Being a part of a mass activity such as this builds up camaraderie among fellow Spartans. They recognize that they are a part of something bigger and better. They are part of a tribe working towards a shared goal.

Today, I am in a group who trained together for a Spartan Race and we still work out together for future races. While grueling and remarkably challenging, being part of a group or a tribe is motivating. Even when they are not around, I find myself thinking of how I eat and how I train on my own. If I don't push myself to my limits, then I would be letting down my tribe.

Because of our accountability to one another, I am motivated to eat well and avoid sugary treats or processed snacks. I use an app on my phone to track the weights I lift at the gym and make it a point to do more reps or more weight on most exercises each week. I needed to simultaneously drop fat and gain muscle on my journey to this Spartan Race. And that sense of accomplishment from crossing the finish line made all the hard work worth it.

Not only has my overall fitness and appearance improved, but my mindset has been shaped by accomplishing this Spartan Race. At the beginning of 2018, I didn't think I was capable of finishing the race. But I trained and ate better and became the man I needed to be to finish it with flying colors.

Once you accomplish something that previously seemed impossible, you view the word very differently. All of life's problems simply become an obstacle to overcome. In training for this event, I pushed past my limits and found I am capable of so much more than I ever imagined.

I climbed a rope for the first time, ran 9 miles in a single session and have even signed up for a half marathon next year. I have plans to run a full marathon after I accomplish that and will go for the Spartan Trifecta by 2020. With the right mindset, anything is possible.

We ran the race as a team, and we worked together to build each other up. We researched technique, nutrition and equipment to better our odds at the race. The Spartan Race creates an all-around healthier and more driven lifestyle. This has literally shaped my year. Because of this event, I have lost 20 pounds in 6 months, gained noticeable muscle mass, and have been living a more fulfilling life. Even though I moved to this town very recently, by joining a tribe working towards a shared goal, I feel connected to the community.

It is funny how so many will make a New Year's resolution but then they completely forget about it after a couple months and move on with their lives focusing on short term pleasure. And while it may be enjoyable to have a fun night, it leads to an unfulfilling life when the fun nights are not complemented with hard work. Conversely, for those who stick with their goals, they find great fulfillment in accomplishing them. Each goal they conquer furthers the winning mindset that they can do more. Each small win can snowball into bigger and bigger wins. From creating a successful Twitter account, to a well-read blog, to a book bought by loyal followers, this year I've shown the amazing progression that follows a man who persists with his goals.

The trick here is to lay the foundation piece by piece. Each piece lays the groundwork for future progress and eventually you look back in wonder at the masterpiece that you built. The problem is seeing the future results when you first start out. It takes a great deal of work ethic, dedication and most importantly, persistence.

AROO! Find your tribe. Find your purpose. Find your motivation.

16. Read Books

Too many people waste their time with Netflix and video games. Reading books will make you more interesting and expand your vocabulary as well as your knowledge. This will also help with your writing. On the days when I can't seem to find the words to contribute to my website, a book I'm working on, or even Twitter, I'll take a few minutes and read from a book.

In fact, on my desk, I keep a few books to consult whenever my day begins to lose direction. Everyone has those days where they can't seem to find the motivation or the direction to conquer their day. That is why I keep these books at the ready: The Meditations by Marcus Aurelius, The Daily Stoic by Ryan Holiday, Tao Te Ching by Lao Tzu and The Art of War by Sun Tzu.

It never ceases to amaze me how reading through the amazing thoughts of someone who took the time and dedication to write a book will inspire me to find my own words. It is infectious in the same way that all forms of media infect us with their energy.

If I lay down to watch TV sitcoms, I'll find myself wasting my time and engaging in more slothful activities. Books, on the other hand, inspire me to live a life more interesting. They inspire me to write down my own thoughts and now I find myself driven to share them with the world.

Set a goal for yourself for this year to read 12 books. It sounds like a lot if you aren't an avid reader, but you'll be amazed at how beneficial this habit can be to your life. The knowledge and perspectives that can be gleaned from books will leave people wondering how you become so knowledgeable and interesting.

Never underestimate how lazy the average person is. Simply reading a book a month will make you stand out in a sea of average. Imagine how interesting you'll be if you manage to take all 20 points from this book and implement them.

Many young men struggle to find the words to begin writing their book or blog. These are the same men whose default activities are porn, Netflix and video games. To write something of interest, you must first live a life of interest. Sitting on the couch and binging on entertainment is no way to light that creative spark inside of you. You have to get out in the real world and find exciting new experiences. If you want to be a writer, you need to study from the greatest who came before you. Read books by Ernest Hemingway, Henry David Thoreau and Robert C. Clark.

Whenever my writing begins to stall out, I take a break and pop open one of the many books that I am currently reading. This will give me the inspiration to write more. It opens my mind to new ways of thinking and provides interesting ideas.

If the book fails to provoke an interesting idea, I simply keep reading. There are worse ways to spend a day than by reading through a classic.

"It is chiefly through books that we enjoy intercourse with superior minds. In the best books, great men talk to us, give us their most precious thoughts and pour their souls into ours."

- William Ellery Channing

17. Meditate

Meditation clears your head and opens your mind. If you think it sounds silly, give it the old college try.

Reaching a meditative state for a few minutes each day can lead to your subconscious delivering new ideas or thoughts to help your mission. Now some days meditation will bear no fruit, but even those sessions provide value. Through these moments of seeking quiet, one can find peace.

In a world growing louder, faster and more stressful, it can be serene to appreciate the occasional sound of silence.

Some of my most original thoughts and ideas come to me when I'm seeking a meditative state. Now, you can always do this by sitting quietly in a room and focusing on nothing. Or you can reach a meditative state by walking through the woods or running down a trail. If you can do a mundane task and focus the mind on nothing, that is meditation.

Everyone has a different method and no method is necessarily better than any other.

Often when I am writing and hit a road block, I'll take a break. Sometimes this means simply calling it quits for the day. Other days I'll go for a walk or meditate for 5 minutes. This allows you to come back to your writing with a fresh mindset and this will often help the words start to flow.

Also, if I find I am getting frustrated or angry with work, or whatever it is, I have found that taking a few minutes to focus on your breathing can really help calm your heart rate. This is beneficial for your health as well as your mindset. When you are operating on an emotional state, you aren't thinking clearly, and this will lead to mistakes. By allowing yourself to slow down and collect yourself, even if it's only a minute, it can save you from overreacting due to emotion.

If you are a smoker, this may help you in stressful situations. I quit smoking two years ago and one issue that I kept running into was I would want a cigarette in a stressful or frustrating situation. Smoking had become my coping mechanism for daily stress and this is an unhealthy habit. One thing that ultimately helped me was meditation.

You can even do this at your job or in school. You don't have to sit in the lotus position. Close your eyes and focus on your breathing while you calm yourself down. This has been an effective replacement for smoking for me. It takes patience, but eventually your body will adapt to this new form of handling stress.

Most people are in too much of a rush throughout their day. They even rush to get to their vacation or weekend. Life is so much more enjoyable when you learn to pace yourself and enjoy the moment. If you're stuck at a Doctor's office, take that as an opportunity to meditate for a few minutes. You could even use this time to contemplate on ideas ruminating in your head. All of this would be more productive and beneficial than mindlessly scrolling through social media.

In my transformation this year, I give a lot of credit to my habit of meditating. It helps me construct new ideas and it heavily influences my writing. Taking a few minutes each day has a profound effect on all 24 hours.

18. No Gossip!

You're not Samantha from Sex and the City. Men don't gossip. Men don't engage others who gossip. If you are a man of purpose, find something more meaningful to talk about.

Ultimately it comes down to having a vision for yourself. You should be focusing your energy and your time on your mission rather than discussing such trivial matters. If you evaluate people who make a hobby out of gossiping, you're likely to find that this person is not truly happy in their life. Therefore they focus on bringing others down to their level rather than raising themselves up.

Every day you have so much mental energy to use. Do not waste this precious commodity. Too many waste their energy on fruitless worries. Do not spread or entertain gossip. When those around you do so, ignore it. Gossip is a waste of time and only small minds engage in it. Gossip robs your mind of time it could use to focus on greater ideas or projects. Men rise above this.

Gossip is essential the supermarket tabloids of the social world. It is cheap in value and easy to do. There is no merit in spreading some raunchy story about a friend or coworker. Nor is there any honor in doing so. Those who do so are typically jealous of the other person or insecure about their own issues.

It ranks below such mundane cookie cutter discussions such as sports and the weather. The sad truth is that most people are living lives so boring or inauthentic to their true desires, that they would rather focus on other people's lives. Its conversational cuckoldry.

People will often relate feelings they experience in conversation with the person communicating. If you are constantly being negative about those around you, expect your peers to look at you with a similar negative light. Conversely, if you focus on the good in people and positive aspects, you'll find that people will think of you in the same positive manner.

19. Stay Off Your Phone When in Company

If you approach a girl and she starts looking at her phone while you are talking to her, walk away. Stop endorsing that disrespectful behavior. She's either not interested or not worth your attention.

If your date checks her phone while you're at dinner, don't call her again. Consider "going to the bathroom" and leaving. This is rude behavior that will only get worse with time.

Leave the phone in your pocket and you'll stand out over the average young person. Be sure to actively listen to the other person; too many people are waiting for their turn to talk. Fun tip: if you don't have anything to say, repeat back part of the last thing the other person said and make it clear you are pondering what was said. This usually will queue a person to expand on what they were saying.

I use this technique all the time, especially if I'm not knowledgeable on the subject. For example:

"I plan on running a Spartan Race next year."

"You're running a Spartan Race?"

"Yeah, I've been training with a group to get ready for all the obstacles."

This gives the other person the opportunity to expand on their thought. This gives you the opportunity to learn more about a topic you may not fully understand. Nearly everyone wants to talk more about their own lives, so this method works 99% of the time.

Moderating your phone use is for all facets of life and not only dates. Wherever you are, make it count. When you go to the gym, be sure to crush your workout. If you are attending school, pay attention so you can learn what is being taught. When you go to work, be a producer. Hell, even when you go to the bar, drink good shit and enjoy your time out with your present company.

Be present in everything you do in your life. This is the secret to life. This may sound a bit new age or Zen for your brash buddy at Path to Manliness, but this mindset is a literal superpower. Your life will greatly improve if you put this into practice.

Enjoy the meal and your company. Enjoy your life.

20. Challenge Yourself

My year has been all about challenging myself to reach new levels. My 2017 was rough and fraught with adversity. Rather than blame the outside forces that led to such a bad year, I am focusing my energy on what I can control, namely, myself.

For 2018 I made a path to a better life. I had a specific outline of goals to accomplish, daily tasks to do and specific habits to ensure a successful year. I woke up before dawn to go on runs. I wrote late at night to finish this book. I was up early in the morning to exercise and edit my writing. I was disciplined with what I ate, and I was consistent with my workouts. I pushed myself farther in my runs. I refused to even think about quitting.

It wasn't easy, and I made a lot sacrifices to fulfill this vision. Along with the great sense of accomplishment I have also created a new me, and a new mindset. In the past I set self-imposed limits on myself via doubt and laziness. That is the old me. The new me challenges myself to topple any obstacle in my way and to constantly push myself to new levels of achievement.

Completing the Spartan Race this year was a transformative experience and it has changed my mindset on life. Now every obstacle in my life is simply something that I will get past. By accomplishing a task that I previously thought to be impossible, I have gained a new sense of confidence in my abilities.

Fortunately for you I have documented what has worked for me in this book. Now it is concise and to the point for a reason. I don't need to bog you down with details when I can be efficient with my words. Reading this book is only the first step. Your challenge now is take what you have learned from me and implement it into your own life and create the life you desire.

With dedication, sacrifice and persistent effort, you will be amazed what you can accomplish in one single year. In 2018, I created my very own website, wrote this book, ran my first 5K and my first Spartan Race. I lost 20 pounds and created the Path to Manliness brand that is reaching out to help young men on their very own paths. What will you do in one year's time?

As Path to Manliness grows, so too will I and its mission. The brand will always focus on helping men live more meaningful lives and coach them on becoming the very best versions they can be. My door is always open, even as it grows bigger than I ever intended.

What can't you do? Build up to it. Run farther. Lift heavier. Write longer. Push yourself past your limits. All of this is meaningless if you don't implement my words into actions. I spent many years paralyzed by fear of failure, but no more.

Now I take action and I no longer fear failure. I simply view failure as critical feedback that leads to future successes. For when I started out on my own Path to Manliness, I made plenty of mistakes.

Fortunately for you, you can learn from many of my mistakes and make new ones on your own. Ha, well, at least you now have the right mindset to stay true to your mission and conquer this life.

Reclaim your manhood!

10 Ways to Gain More Twitter Followers

1. Tweet our good content consistently. You need to be tweeting every day, preferably several times each day.

2. Reply to popular tweets. When you first start out you have so few followers, so it will be difficult to get noticed. Find people who have decent followers and comment on their tweets. This can "borrow" their audience and get more likes.

3. Follow people who like your comments. When people like or retweet your comments, give them a follow. If they like that comment, they will like other tweets you write.

4. Give out likes and follows. One good way to get noticed is to like another user's tweets. Aim for people with lower follower counts as they are more likely to notice your like than a person who gets 100 likes on each tweet.

5. Find someone who writes similar stuff to you. Follow people who like and retweet their stuff. Engage with them in conversation. They will probably like and retweet your content if you write good content that is similar. These are also going to be the more active followers. This is the most effective tip to grow your following.

6. Get a picture. You need to have something up there to catch people's attention. This is your logo, or your face. Whatever it is, it is the image that people will associate with you.

7. Write a good bio! This one is huge, and few people can come up with anything decent here. But this is where people get the first impression of what your account is about. Be funny or throw some buzzwords up there to help people decide what you're about.

8. Be engaged with the community. Reply, like, retweet stuff on occasion. Quote tweets and add your thoughts to it. This one is big as it will often get retweeted if done right. It gives the other person a chance to retweet you and themselves. Even as my account has grown very large, I still do my best to respond to people. I enjoy the interaction.

9. Pictures. They grab your audiences' eyes and stand out among the plain words. I rather use words but try and tweet at least one picture a day. Don't overthink this. Sometimes the dumbest stuff will gain traction.

10. Be authentic. Be you. It will be difficult to maintain a person that is not natural, and people will see through it. So be sure to be honest and live the life you share. And be sure to share personal experiences. People like to remember that they are talking to a fellow human, not a bot.

Thank you to all the following who have shown support to Path to Manliness!

Jack W. Parks

@ThePrizeAwaits

Lastly, I want to thank you for buying this book. I put a lot of thought, time and effort into Reclaim Your Manhood and I didn't do it for the money. I didn't do it for fame. I did it to help people.

I genuinely hope everyone who buys this book enjoys it, and I hope they are able to implement my words into action in their own lives.

As I write these words, it is a bit surreal to think that I wrote my first book, but I truly enjoyed the experience. If it is well received, I plan on working on another book in 2019.

If I've inspired you in anyway, please let me know. Message me on twitter or write me an email. I do read my DMs. I do check my email. I would love to hear from you and if I can help you in any way, I will do what I can. If you would like to help me out, please write a review of this book. As a new author, this will help me out tremendously. If you know someone who can benefit from my advice, tell them about this book.

Thank you for reading it. I sense great things ahead for the Path to Manliness brand and I look forward to seeing what comes forth from those who have been inspired by my words.

This is your life. Reclaim it.

Made in the USA
San Bernardino,
CA